foreword

At Company's Coming we think bananas are tops! They are low in fat and a great source of vitamin C and potassium—plus, they can be enjoyed in all kinds of dishes, whether they're still green or too ripe to be taken for lunch. And we've gathered a bunch of our recipes to prove it!

For best results, choose the right banana for the job. Treats like Bacon-Wrapped Bananas require firm, underripe bananas. Deliciously savoury Banana and Pineapple Chutney works with the perfectly in-between ones. And if you're hankering to bake some Banana PB Muffins, use up those overripe bananas chilling out in the freezer.

Enjoy bananas in breakfast baking, savoury main courses or decadent desserts—explore all your options with this friendly, nutritious fruit!

Jean Paré

sunrise beverage

A special drink to help welcome the day. This banana and peach combination creates a beautiful layered "sunrise."

Can of frozen concentrated peach punch	12 1/2 oz.	355 mL
Water	2 cups	500 mL
Lemon juice	2 tbsp.	30 mL
Frozen large bananas, cut into 4 pieces each	2	2
Ice cubes	24	24
Grenadine syrup	1/2 cup	125 mL
Orange slices	6	6
Maraschino cherries	6	6

Process first 4 ingredients in blender for about 30 seconds until smooth. Remove and set aside half of mixture.

Add half of ice cubes through hole in lid of blender, 1 at a time, processing after each addition until smooth. Pour into large pitcher. Process remaining peach mixture and ice cubes. Add to pitcher.

Pour 4 tsp. (20 mL) grenadine into bottom of six 14 oz. (398 mL) glasses. Add peach mixture until glasses are 3/4 full. Stir gently in bottom of glass to achieve sunrise appearance.

Garnish with orange slice and cherry skewered on cocktail pick. Serves 6.

1 serving: 150 Calories; 0 g Total Fat (0 g Mono, 0 g Poly, 0 g Sat); 0 mg Cholesterol; 37 g Carbohydrate; 1 g Fibre; trace Protein; 10 mg Sodium

dressed-up fruit cups

This versatile treat can be served up any time of the day!

CINNAMON WALNUTS

Walnut pieces	1/2 cup	125 mL
Brown sugar, packed	1 tbsp.	15 mL
Ground cinnamon	1/4 tsp.	1 mL
Medium navel oranges, peeled, quartered lengthwise and sliced	3	3
Medium unpeeled cooking apple (such as McIntosh), finely diced	1	1
Medium bananas, quartered lengthwise and cut into thick slices	2	2
Kiwi fruit, quartered lengthwise and sliced	2	2
Seedless red grapes, halved	1 cup	250 mL

HONEY YOGURT SAUCE

Non-fat vanilla (or plain) yogurt	1 cup	250 mL
Liquid honey	1/4 cup	60 mL
Vanilla extract (optional)	1/4 tsp.	1 mL
Grated lemon (or orange) zest (optional)	1/4 tsp.	1 mL

Cinnamon Walnuts: Wash walnuts with hot water. Drain. Blot with paper towel to remove excess moisture. Walnuts will still be damp.

Combine brown sugar and cinnamon in small bowl. Add walnuts. Toss until coated. Spread evenly on foil-lined baking sheet with sides. Bake in 400°F (200°C) oven for about 10 minutes until browned and toasted. Cool.

Combine next 5 ingredients in large bowl. Spoon into 6 bowls.

Honey Yogurt Sauce: Whisk all 4 ingredients in small bowl. Makes about 1 cup (250 mL) sauce. Drizzle over fruit. Sprinkle with walnut mixture. Makes 6 fruit cups.

1 fruit cup: 277 Calories; 8.1 g Total Fat (1.1 g Mono, 5.1 g Poly, 1.1 g Sat); 2 mg Cholesterol; 51 g Carbohydrate; 5 g Fibre; 5 g Protein; 32 mg Sodium

breakfast split

A breakfast-friendly version of an ice cream shoppe favourite. Customize by replacing the berries with equal amounts of fresh or canned fruit of your choice.

Vanilla frozen yogurt	3/4 cup	175 mL
Medium banana	1	1
Chopped fresh strawberries	1/4 cup	60 mL
Fresh raspberries	1/4 cup	60 mL
Granola	1/4 cup	60 mL

Put frozen yogurt into serving bowl.

Cut the banana in half crosswise. Cut both halves lengthwise into 2 pieces, for a total of 4 pieces. Arrange around frozen yogurt.

Sprinkle with remaining 3 ingredients. Serves 1.

1 serving: 472 Calories; 13.4 g Total Fat (3.6 g Mono, 5 g Poly, 4.2 g Sat); 11 mg Cholesterol; 82 g Carbohydrate; 7 g Fibre; 14 g Protein; 117 mg Sodium

banana fritters

A delectable treat akin to carnival fare! Try serving it with vanilla ice cream.

All-purpose flour	1 cup	250 mL
Baking powder	2 tsp.	10 mL
Baking soda	1/4 tsp.	1 mL
Water	1 1/4 cups	300 mL
Medium bananas, cut into 3 inch (7.5 cm) pieces	4	4
All-purpose flour	2 tbsp.	30 mL
Cooking oil, for deep-frying		
CARAMEL SAUCE		
Water	1/3 cup	75 mL
Cornstarch	1 tbsp.	15 mL
Brown sugar, packed	1 cup	250 mL
Whipping cream	1/2 cup	125 mL
Hard margarine (or butter)	1/3 cup	75 mL

Combine first 3 ingredients in large bowl. Make a well in centre.

Add water to well. Stir until batter is smooth.

Put bananas into medium bowl. Sprinkle with second amount of flour. Toss gently until coated. Dip banana pieces, 1 at a time, into batter. Deep-fry, in 2 to 3 batches, in hot (350°F, 175°C) cooking oil for 3 to 5 minutes until golden brown. Transfer to plate lined with paper towel to drain.

Caramel Sauce: Stir water into cornstarch in medium saucepan. Add next 3 ingredients. Heat and stir on medium-high for 5 to 10 minutes until boiling and thickened. Makes about 1 1/2 cups (375 mL) sauce. Drizzle over banana fritters. Serves 4.

1 serving: 767 Calories; 34 g Total Fat (17.6 g Mono, 4.2 g Poly, 10.4 g Sat); 37 mg Cholesterol; 115 g Carbohydrate; 3 g Fibre; 6 g Protein; 489 mg Sodium

bacon-wrapped bananas

Sweet and salty go hand in hand! This pairing may seem unusual, but it is delicious.

Bacon slices	16	16
Dijon mustard (with whole seeds)	4 tsp.	20 mL
Pepper, sprinkle		
Underripe large bananas	2	2

Cook bacon in medium frying pan on medium-high for about 4 minutes until almost crisp. Drain.

Spread about 1/4 tsp. (1 mL) mustard on each bacon slice. Sprinkle with pepper.

Cut each banana into 8 pieces. Wrap 1 bacon slice, mustard-side in, around each banana chunk, securing with cocktail pick. Place on rack in broiler pan. Broil on centre rack in oven for 3 to 4 minutes, turning occasionally, until bacon is crisp. Transfer to paper towel-lined plate to drain. Serve warm. Makes 16 appetizers.

1 appetizer: 50 Calories; 3.2 g Total Fat (1.5 g Mono, 0.4 g Poly, 1.1 g Sat); 5 mg Cholesterol; 4 g Carbohydrate; trace Fibre; 2 g Protein; 116 mg Sodium

jamaican chicken salad

Brown sugar, packed	2 tsp.	10 mL
Dried thyme, crushed	1 tsp.	5 mL
Ground allspice	1/2 tsp.	2 mL
Cayenne pepper	1/4 – 1 tsp.	1 mL
Ground nutmeg	1/4 tsp.	1 mL
Salt	1/4 tsp.	1 mL
Coarsely ground pepper, sprinkle		
Ground cloves, sprinkle		
Boneless, skinless chicken breast halves (4–6 oz., 113–170 g, each)	3	3
Cooking oil	3 tbsp.	45 mL
Firm, slightly green banana, peeled and halved lengthwise	1	1
Canned pineapple slices	19 oz.	540 mL
Medium red pepper, quartered	1	1
Liquid honey	1/4 cup	60 mL
Reserved pineapple juice	1/4 cup	60 mL
Lime juice	2 tbsp.	30 mL
Avocado, peeled and diced	1	1
Shredded lettuce, lightly packed	6 cups	1.5 L

Combine first 8 ingredients in small bowl. Pound chicken breasts to even thickness. Sprinkle both sides with 1 tbsp. (15 mL) brown sugar mixture. Let stand for 10 minutes.

Combine remaining brown sugar mixture with cooking oil. Brush over banana, pineapple slices and red peppers, and place them on greased grill preheated to medium. Close lid. Cook for 5 to 15 minutes, turning several times, until soft. Cut banana into chunks, pineapple into quarters and red pepper into slivers. Transfer to large bowl. Grill chicken for 20 to 25 minutes until internal temperature reaches 170°F (77°C). Transfer to cutting board. Cut into slivers. Add to fruit mixture. Toss.

Combine next 3 ingredients in small bowl. Add avocado. Toss until coated. Pour over chicken mixture. Divide lettuce among 4 salad plates. Spoon warm chicken mixture over top. Serves 4.

1 serving: 460 Calories; 19 g Total Fat (11 g Mono, 4 g Poly, 2.5 g Sat); 50 mg Cholesterol; 54 g Carbohydrate; 8 g Fibre; 23 g Protein; 210 mg Sodium

fruited lamb curry

Delectably tender lamb with the sweetness of banana and pineapple.

Cooking oil	1 tbsp.	15 mL
Boneless lamb shoulder, trimmed of fat and cut into 1 1/2 inch (3.8 cm) cubes	2 lbs.	900 g
Seasoned salt	1 tsp.	5 mL
Pepper, sprinkle		
Coarsely chopped onion	1 1/2 cups	375 mL
Curry paste	2 tsp.	10 mL
Garlic cloves, crushed	2	2
Ground coriander	1/4 tsp.	1 mL
Ground ginger	1/4 tsp.	1 mL
Can of coconut milk	14 oz.	398 mL
Reserved juice from pineapple tidbits		
Can of pineapple tidbits, drained and juice reserved	14 oz.	398 mL
Underripe bananas, cut into 1/2 inch (12 mm) slices	2	2
Water	2 tbsp.	30 mL
Lemon juice	1 tbsp.	15 mL
Cornstarch	1 tbsp.	15 mL
Slivered almonds, toasted (see Tip, page 64)	1/4 cup	60 mL

Heat cooking oil in large frying pan on medium-high. Cook lamb in batches, turning occasionally, until browned. Sprinkle with seasoned salt and pepper. Transfer to paper towel-lined plate to drain.

Add next 5 ingredients to same frying pan. Cook, stirring occasionally, until onion is softened. Add coconut milk and reserved pineapple juice. Stir. Add lamb. Simmer, covered, for 1 to 1 1/2 hours until lamb is tender.

Add pineapple and banana. Stir. Stir water and lemon juice into cornstarch in small bowl. Add to lamb mixture. Heat and stir for about 5 minutes until boiling and slightly thickened. Sprinkle with almonds. Makes about 6 1/2 cups (1.6 L).

1 serving: 460 Calories; 25 g Total Fat (5 g Mono, 1.5 g Poly, 16 g Sat); 95 mg Cholesterol; 30 g Carbohydrate; 3 g Fibre; 33 g Protein; 540 mg Sodium

philippines stew

Bananas give this spicy, hearty blend an especially tropical flavour.

Sausage meat	1/2 lb.	225 g
Chopped onion	1 1/2 cups	375 mL
Garlic cloves, minced	3	3
Finely chopped ginger root	2 tsp.	10 mL
Cayenne pepper	1/4 tsp.	1 mL
Cubed sweet potato (about 1 lb., 454 g)	3 cups	750 mL
Low-sodium prepared chicken broth	3 cups	750 mL
Stewed tomatoes, with juice	2 cups	500 mL
Boneless, skinless chicken breast halves, cut into 1 1/2 inch (3.8 cm) pieces	1 lb.	454 g
Chickpeas (garbanzo beans)	1 1/2 cups	375 mL
Converted white rice	1 cup	250 mL
Bay leaf	1	1
Sliced bok choy (about 2 medium)	4 cups	1 L
Underripe bananas, sliced 1/2 inch (12 mm) thick	2	2
Green onions, thinly sliced	4	4

Scramble-fry sausage in Dutch oven or large pot until browned. Drain. Rinse with warm water. Drain. Return to pot.

Add next 3 ingredients. Heat and stir on medium-high for about 5 minutes until onion is soft. Sprinkle with cayenne pepper. Stir.

Add next 7 ingredients. Stir. Bring to a boil. Reduce heat to medium-low. Simmer, covered, for about 40 minutes, stirring occaisionally, until rice is tender. Remove and discard bay leaf.

Add next 3 ingredients. Stir. Cook, covered, for 5 to 10 minutes until heated through. Makes about 12 cups (3 L). Serves 6.

1 serving: 560 Calories; 14 g Total Fat (6 g Mono, 2 g Poly, 4.5 g Sat); 75 mg Cholesterol; 74 g Carbohydrate; 9 g Fibre; 35 g Protein; 1130 mg Sodium

banana pineapple chutney

This chutney pairs well with any grilled meat. Hot peppers contain capsaicin in the seeds and ribs. Removing the seeds and ribs will reduce the heat. Wear rubber gloves when handling hot peppers, and avoid touching your eyes. Wash your hands well afterwards.

Medium bananas, halved lengthwise and cut into 1 inch (2.5 cm) pieces	2	2
Chopped fresh pineapple (about 1/2 inch, 12 mm, pieces)	1 cup	250 mL
Brown sugar, packed	1/4 cup	60 mL
Dark (navy) rum	1/4 cup	60 mL
Malt vinegar	2 tbsp.	30 mL
Finely chopped fresh (or sliced pickled) jalapeño pepper	2 tsp.	10 mL
Salt	1/2 tsp.	2 mL
Ground cardamom	1/8 tsp.	0.5 mL

Combine all 8 ingredients in large saucepan. Cook on medium-high for 10 to 15 minutes, stirring occasionally, until banana is soft and mixture is thickened. Makes about 1 1/2 cups (375 mL).

__2 tbsp. (30 mL):__ 41 Calories; 0.2 g Total Fat (trace Mono, trace Poly, trace Sat); 0 mg Cholesterol; 10 g Carbohydrate; 1 g Fibre; trace Protein; 78 mg Sodium

banana pancakes

This delicious weekend treat is perfect for banana lovers! Feel free to make these pancakes with strawberry, white or chocolate milk in place of the banana milk.

Pancake mix	1 1/4 cups	300 mL
Large egg, fork-beaten	1	1
Banana-flavoured milk	1 cup	250 mL
Peanut butter	2 tbsp.	30 mL
Medium bananas, sliced	2	2

Put pancake mix into large bowl. Make a well in centre.

Combine next 3 ingredients in small bowl. Add to well. Stir until just moistened. Batter will be lumpy.

Heat 1 tsp. (5 mL) cooking oil in large frying pan on medium-low. Pour batter into pan, using about 1/4 cup (60 mL) for each pancake. Cook for about 3 minutes until bubbles form on top and edges appear dry. Turn pancakes over. Cook for 2 to 3 minutes until bottoms are golden. Use the lifter to check. Transfer to large plate. Cover to keep warm. Repeat with remaining batter, heating more cooking oil in the pan before each batch if necessary to prevent sticking. Makes 8 pancakes. Place 1 pancake on each of 4 plates. Cover with banana slices. Top with remaining pancakes. Serves 4.

1 serving: *339 Calories; 11.9 g Total Fat (5.5 g Mono, 3.1 g Poly, 2.4 g Sat); 66 mg Cholesterol; 49 g Carbohydrate; 3 g Fibre; 11 g Protein; 609 mg Sodium*

amaranth banana bread

Tired of the same old banana bread? Amaranth is a unique and healthy whole-grain addition that you must try.

All-purpose flour	2 cups	500 mL
Ground cinnamon	1 1/2 tsp.	7 mL
Baking powder	1 tsp.	5 mL
Baking soda	1 tsp.	5 mL
Salt	1/2 tsp.	2 mL
Butter (or hard margarine), softened	1/3 cup	75 mL
Granulated sugar	3/4 cup	175 mL
Cooked amaranth (see Tip, page 64)	1 cup	250 mL
Mashed overripe banana (about 2 large)	1 cup	250 mL
Large eggs, fork-beaten	2	2
Buttermilk (or soured milk, see Tip, page 64)	1/2 cup	125 mL

Combine first 5 ingredients in large bowl. Stir. Make a well in centre.

Beat butter and sugar in medium bowl until light and creamy.

Add amaranth and banana. Mix until no clumps of amaranth remain. Add eggs and buttermilk. Beat well. Add to well. Stir until just moistened. Spread evenly in greased 9 x 5 x 3 inch (23 x 12.5 x 7.5 cm) loaf pan. Bake in 375°F (190°C) oven for 1 hour. Wooden pick inserted in centre may still show some moistness, but loaf should be cracked on top and firm to the touch. Let stand in pan for 10 minutes before removing to wire rack to cool. Cuts into 16 slices.

1 slice: 195 Calories; 5.3 g Total Fat (1.4 g Mono, 0.7 g Poly, 2.8 g Sat); 33 mg Cholesterol; 33 g Carbohydrate; 3 g Fibre; 5 g Protein; 213 mg Sodium

banana ginger muffins

These muffins are a bit healthier than average as they contain oats and whole-wheat flour, and are sweetened with maple syrup. A hint of spicy ginger completes the flavour.

All-purpose flour	1 1/2 cups	375 mL
Brown sugar, packed	1/2 cup	125 mL
Quick-cooking rolled oats	1/2 cup	125 mL
Whole-wheat flour	1/3 cup	75 mL
Minced crystallized ginger	3 tbsp.	45 mL
Baking powder	1 tbsp.	15 mL
Large egg, fork-beaten	1	1
Buttermilk (or soured milk, see Tip, page 64)	1 1/4 cups	300 mL
Mashed banana (about 2 large)	1 cup	250 mL
Maple (or maple-flavoured) syrup	1/4 cup	60 mL
Cooking oil	2 tbsp.	30 mL
Brown sugar, packed	3 tbsp.	45 mL

Combine first 6 ingredients in large bowl. Make a well in centre.

Combine next 5 ingredients in medium bowl. Add to well. Stir until just moistened. Do not overmix.

Fill 12 greased muffin cups 3/4 full. Sprinkle with second amount of brown sugar. Bake in 375°F (190°C) oven for 20 to 25 minutes until wooden pick inserted in centre of muffin comes out clean. Let stand in pan for 5 minutes before removing to wire rack to cool. Makes 12 muffins.

1 muffin: 215 Calories; 3.5 g Total Fat (1.7 g Mono, 0.9 g Poly, 0.6 g Sat); 19 mg Cholesterol; 43 g Carbohydrate; 2 g Fibre; 4 g Protein; 164 mg Sodium

banana chip muffins

Tasty muffins starring the timeless combination of banana and chocolate—
they'll be loved by kids and grown-ups alike.

All-purpose flour	1 cup	250 mL
Quick-cooking rolled oats	1 cup	250 mL
Whole-wheat flour	2/3 cup	150 mL
Brown sugar, packed	1/4 cup	60 mL
Baking powder	2 tsp.	10 mL
Baking soda	1 tsp.	5 mL
Ground cinnamon	1/2 tsp.	2 mL
Salt	1/2 tsp.	2 mL
Mashed banana (about 3 large)	1 1/2 cups	375 mL
Buttermilk (or soured milk, see Tip, page 64)	2/3 cup	150 mL
Large egg, fork-beaten	1	1
Cooking oil	1/4 cup	60 mL
Mini semi-sweet chocolate chips	2/3 cup	150 mL

Combine first 8 ingredients in large bowl. Make a well in centre.

Whisk next 4 ingredients together in medium bowl. Add to well.

Add chocolate chips. Stir until just moistened. Fill 12 greased muffin cups
3/4 full. Bake in 375°F (190°C) oven for about 20 minutes until wooden pick
inserted in centre of muffin comes out clean. Let stand in pan for
5 minutes before removing to wire rack to cool. Makes 12 muffins.

1 muffin: 246 Calories; 9.3 g Total Fat (4.3 g Mono, 1.9 g Poly, 2.5 g Sat); 18 mg Cholesterol;
38 g Carbohydrate; 3 g Fibre; 5 g Protein; 292 mg Sodium

banana pb muffins

Your favourite sandwich fixings in muffin form—with a little chocolate thrown in too! Make them with your preferred peanut butter, whether chunky or smooth.

All-purpose flour	1 cup	250 mL
Whole-wheat flour	1 cup	250 mL
Brown sugar, packed	1/3 cup	75 mL
Baking powder	1 tbsp.	15 mL
Salt	1/2 tsp.	2 mL
Large egg, fork-beaten	1	1
Mashed overripe banana (about 2 medium)	3/4 cup	175 mL
Peanut butter	2/3 cup	150 mL
Vanilla (or plain) soy milk	2/3 cup	150 mL
Cooking oil	2 tbsp.	30 mL
Mini semi-sweet chocolate chips	1/2 cup	125 mL

Combine first 5 ingredients in large bowl. Stir. Make a well in centre.

Beat next 5 ingredients with whisk in medium bowl. Add to well.

Add chocolate chips. Stir until just moistened. Fill 12 greased muffin cups 3/4 full. Bake in 375°F (190°C) oven for 18 to 20 minutes until wooden pick inserted in centre of muffin comes out clean. Let stand in pan for 5 minutes before removing to wire rack to cool. Makes 12 muffins.

1 muffin: 270 Calories; 13.2 g Total Fat (5.9 g Mono, 3.3 g Poly, 3.2 g Sat); 18 mg Cholesterol; 34 g Carbohydrate; 3 g Fibre; 8 g Protein; 276 mg Sodium

banana cake

Keep one of these moist cakes in the freezer in case company drops by. The cinnamon-spiced cake is topped with cream cheese icing that has a hint of orange flavour.

Butter (or hard margarine), softened	1/2 cup	125 mL
Granulated sugar	2/3 cup	150 mL
Large eggs	2	2
Medium bananas, mashed	3	3
Milk	2 tbsp.	30 mL
All-purpose flour	1 1/2 cups	375 mL
Baking powder	1 tbsp.	15 mL
Ground cinnamon	1 tsp.	5 mL
CREAM CHEESE ICING		
Cream cheese, softened	4 oz.	125 g
Butter (or hard margarine), softened	2 tbsp.	30 mL
Icing (confectioner's) sugar	1 1/2 cups	375 mL
Grated orange zest	1 tsp.	5 mL

Beat butter and sugar in large bowl until light and creamy. Add eggs, 1 at a time, beating well after each addition. Add banana and milk. Beat well.

Combine next 3 ingredients in medium bowl. Add to banana mixture. Stir until just moistened. Spread evenly in greased 8 inch (20 cm) springform pan. Bake in 350°F (175°C) oven for about 45 minutes until wooden pick inserted in centre comes out clean. Let stand in pan for 5 minutes before removing to wire rack to cool.

Cream Cheese Icing: Beat cream cheese and butter in separate medium bowl until smooth.

Add icing sugar and zest. Beat well. Spread evenly over top of cake. Cuts into 12 wedges.

1 wedge: 334 Calories; 14.8 g Total Fat (7.9 g Mono, 1.3 g Poly, 4.7 g Sat); 47 mg Cholesterol; 48 g Carbohydrate; 1 g Fibre; 4 g Protein; 253 mg Sodium

chocolate banana cake

Semi-sweet chocolate baking squares (1 oz., 28 g, each), chopped	4	4
Butter	1/4 cup	60 mL
All-purpose flour	1 1/2 cups	375 mL
Granulated sugar	3/4 cup	175 mL
Baking powder	2 tsp.	10 mL
Instant coffee granules	2 tsp.	10 mL
Salt	1/2 tsp.	2 mL
Buttermilk (see Tip, page 64)	1 cup	250 mL
Small banana, mashed	1	1
Large eggs, fork-beaten	2	2
CHOCOLATE GLAZE		
Whipping cream	1/2 cup	125 mL
Semi-sweet chocolate baking squares (1 oz., 28 g, each), chopped	4	4

Heat chocolate and butter in small heavy saucepan on lowest heat, stirring often, until chocolate is almost melted. Do not overheat. Remove from heat. Stir until smooth. Set aside.

Combine next 5 ingredients in large bowl. Make a well in centre.

Combine next 3 ingredients in small bowl. Add to well. Beat until smooth. Add chocolate mixture. Stir. Line bottom of greased 9 inch (23 cm) round pan with waxed paper. Spread batter evenly in pan. Bake in 350°F (175°C) oven for about 40 minutes until wooden pick inserted in centre comes out clean. Let stand in pan on wire rack for 10 minutes. Remove cake to wire rack to cool, discarding waxed paper from bottom of cake. Set rack in waxed paper-lined baking sheet with sides.

Chocolate Glaze: Heat whipping cream in heavy medium saucepan on medium-low until bubbles start to form around edge. Do not boil. Remove from heat. Add chocolate. Stir until mixture is smooth. Let stand for 5 minutes. Spread over top and side of cake, allowing excess to drip off. Chill for at least 30 minutes. Cuts into 12 wedges.

1 wedge: *298 Calories; 14.3 g Total Fat (4.4 g Mono, 0.6 g Poly, 8.4 g Sat); 60 mg Cholesterol; 41 g Carbohydrate; 2 g Fibre; 5 g Protein; 242 mg Sodium*

pineapple banana cheesecake

This cheesecake may taste rich, but it is an almost guiltless dessert!

Flaked coconut	3/4 cup	175 mL
All-purpose flour	1/4 cup	60 mL
Cooking oil	2 tbsp.	30 mL
Low-fat cottage	2 cups	500 mL
Blocks of light cream cheese	2	2
(8 oz., 250 g, each), softened, cubed		
Granulated sugar	1 cup	250 mL
Cornstarch	3 tbsp.	45 mL
Ripe medium bananas, cut up	2	2
Egg whites (large)	3	3
Large egg	1	1
Granulated sugar	1/4 cup	60 mL
Cornstarch	1 tbsp.	15 mL
Can of crushed pineapple (with juice)	14 oz.	398 mL

Combine coconut and flour in small bowl. Slowly drizzle with cooking oil, while tossing with fork, until well distributed. Spray bottom of 9 inch (23 cm) springform pan with cooking spray. Press coconut mixture firmly into bottom. Bake in 350°F (175°C) oven for about 10 minutes until lightly golden. Cool. Spray sides of pan with cooking spray. Press strips of waxed paper, 2 inches (5 cm) wide and a total of 30 inches (76 cm) long, to side of pan.

Put next 3 ingredients into food processor. Process for about 1 minute until smooth. Add cornstarch and banana. Pulse with on/off motion until banana is broken up. Process for about 1 minute until smooth. Add egg whites and egg. Process for 5 seconds. Pour over crust. Bake in 450°F (230°C) oven for 10 minutes. Reduce heat to 250°F (120°C). Bake for about 1 1/2 hours until surface appears solid but centre still wobbles slightly. Let stand in pan on wire rack until set and cooled.

Combine sugar and cornstarch in small saucepan. Add pineapple with juice. Stir. Heat and stir on medium until boiling and slightly thickened. Cool for 15 minutes. Spread evenly over cheesecake. Chill until cold. Remove side of pan. Remove and discard waxed paper. Cuts into 12 wedges.

1 wedge: 321 Calories; 12.0 g Total Fat (1.7 g Mono, 0.8 g Poly, 7.1 g Sat); 39 mg Cholesterol; 41 g Carbohydrate; 1 g Fibre; 11 g Protein; 400 mg Sodium

coconut banana cheesecake

A delicious cheesecake with tropical flavours—the perfect ending to a low-key weekend meal.

CRUST

Butter (or hard margarine), melted	2/3 cup	150 mL
Graham cracker crumbs	1 2/3 cups	400 mL
Medium coconut, toasted (see Tip, page 64)	2/3 cup	150 mL

FILLING

Cream cheese, softened	16 oz.	500 g
Brown sugar, packed	1/2 cup	125 mL
Large eggs, fork-beaten	3	3
Mashed banana (about 3 large)	1 1/2 cups	375 mL
Medium coconut, toasted	2/3 cup	150 mL
Dark (navy) rum	3 tbsp.	45 mL
Lime juice	2 tbsp.	30 mL

TOPPING

Whipping cream (or 2 cups, 500 mL, frozen whipped topping, thawed)	1 cup	250 mL
Flaked coconut, toasted	2 tbsp.	30 mL
Lime slices	12	12

Crust: Combine first 3 ingredients in medium bowl. Press into bottom and 3/4 up side of greased 9 inch (23 cm) springform pan lined with waxed paper. Chill for 1 hour.

Filling: Beat cream cheese and brown sugar in large bowl until smooth. Add next 5 ingredients. Beat until well combined. Pour mixture over crust. Place pan on baking sheet. Bake in 350°F (175°C) oven for about 50 minutes until set. Turn oven off. Cool in oven with door ajar for 1 hour. Chill for at least 4 hours or overnight.

Topping: Beat whipping cream in medium bowl until soft peaks form. Spread over top of cheesecake. Sprinkle with coconut. Arrange lime slices around outside edge. Cuts into 12 wedges.

1 wedge: 504 Calories; 38.8 g Total Fat (14.4 g Mono, 2.2 g Poly, 20 g Sat); 124 mg Cholesterol; 34 g Carbohydrate; 1 g Fibre; 7 g Protein; 382 mg Sodium

banana butterscotch cream pie

This low-fat cream pie can be prepped in less than half an hour. Just chill and enjoy!

CRUST

Vanilla wafer crumbs	1 1/2 cups	375 mL
Butter (or hard margarine), melted	2 tbsp.	30 mL

FILLING

Brown sugar, packed	1/4 cup	60 mL
All-purpose flour	2 tbsp.	30 mL
Cornstarch	2 tbsp.	30 mL
Salt	1/2 tsp.	2 mL
Skim milk	1 cup	250 mL
Skim evaporated milk	1 cup	250 mL
Frozen egg product, thawed	1/3 cup	75 mL
Vanilla extract	1 tsp.	5 mL
Butterscotch extract	1 tsp.	5 mL
Medium bananas, sliced	2	2

Frozen light whipped topping, thawed,
    for garnish
Sliced bananas, for garnish

Crust: Combine wafer crumbs and butter in small bowl. Reserve 2 tbsp. (30 mL) crumb mixture in small cup for topping. Press remaining crumb mixture into bottom of lightly greased 9 inch (23 cm) pie plate. Bake in 350°F (175°C) oven for 10 minutes. Let stand until cool.

Filling: Combine first 4 ingredients in medium saucepan. Slowly add skim and evaporated milk, stirring constantly with whisk. Heat and stir on medium until boiling and thickened. Remove from heat.

Slowly add egg product, stirring constantly with whisk. Heat and stir on low for 2 minutes. Remove from heat. Add vanilla and butterscotch extract. Add banana. Stir gently. Pour into crust. Sprinkle with reserved crumb mixture. Cover with plastic wrap directly on surface to prevent skin from forming. Cool. Chill until cold.

Garnish with whipped topping and banana. Cuts into 8 wedges.

1 wedge: 250 Calories; 8 g Total Fat (2 g Mono, 3 g Poly, 2 g Sat); 5 mg Cholesterol; 40 g Carbohydrate; trace Fibre; 5 g Protein; 320 mg Sodium

crisp meringue cream pies

Adorable little meringue pies filled with creamy banana custard. Serve up a healthier take on banana cream pie!

Egg whites (large), room temperature	6	6
Granulated sugar	1 1/2 cups	375 mL
Granulated sugar	1/2 cup	125 mL
Custard powder	1/4 cup	60 mL
All-purpose flour	2 tbsp.	30 mL
Milk	3/4 cup	175 mL
Can of skim evaporated milk	13 1/2 oz.	385 mL
Vanilla (or banana) extract	1 tsp.	5 mL
Diced banana	1 1/2 cups	375 mL
Gingersnaps, crushed	2	2

Beat egg whites in large bowl until soft peaks form. Add first amount of sugar, 1 tbsp. (15 mL) at a time, beating constantly until stiff peaks form and sugar is dissolved. Line bottom of baking sheet with parchment (not waxed) paper. Trace eight 3 inch (7.5 cm) circles, about 2 inches (5 cm) apart, on paper. Turn paper over. Spoon meringue into piping bag fitted with star tip. Pipe onto circles, filling each circle completely and building sides to about 2 inches (5 cm) high. Bake on centre rack in 200°F (95°C) oven for 2 to 3 hours until dry. Turn oven off. Let meringues stand in oven with door ajar until cool. Remove meringues to wire rack.

Combine next 3 ingredients in medium saucepan. Slowly stir in milk and evaporated milk until smooth. Heat and stir on medium until boiling and thickened. Reduce heat to medium-low. Cook for 1 minute. Remove from heat.

Stir in vanilla and banana. Cover with plastic wrap directly on surface to prevent skin from forming. Cool. Spoon about 1/2 cup (125 mL) banana mixture into meringues.

Sprinkle with gingersnap crumbs. Serve within 1 hour. Makes 8 pies.

1 pie: 324 Calories; 0.6 g Total Fat (0.2 g Mono, 0.1 g Poly, 0.3 g Sat); 1 mg Cholesterol; 74 g Carbohydrate; 1 g Fibre; 7 g Protein; 130 mg Sodium

banana cream pie

The perfect banana cream pie. Creamy and rich, yet not overly sweet. Simple and delicious.

Box of instant vanilla pudding powder (6-serving size)	1	1
Milk	1 cup	250 mL
Frozen whipped topping, thawed	1 cup	250 mL
Medium bananas, sliced	2	2
Chocolate (or graham cracker) crumb crust (9 inch, 22 cm, diameter)	1	1
Frozen whipped topping, thawed	1 cup	250 mL
Banana chips, for garnish		

Beat pudding powder and milk in medium bowl until smooth.

Fold in first amount of whipped topping and banana. Spread evenly in crumb crust.

Spread second amount of whipped topping evenly over pudding mixture.

Garnish with banana chips. Cuts into 8 wedges.

1 wedge: 285 Calories; 11.9 g Total Fat (3.6 g Mono, 2.1 g Poly, 5.8 g Sat); 2 mg Cholesterol; 44 g Carbohydrate; 1 g Fibre; 3 g Protein; 381 mg Sodium

cinnamon banana boats

Bananas, cinnamon and caramel are a perfect match in these appealing little wraps.

Small bananas, trimmed to 4 inches (10 cm) each	4	4
Flour tortillas (6 inch, 15 cm, diameter)	4	4
Granulated sugar	1/4 cup	60 mL
Ground cinnamon	2 tsp.	10 mL
Butter, melted	1/4 cup	60 mL
Caramel Irish cream liqueur	3 tbsp.	45 mL
Chocolate hazelnut spread	3 tbsp.	45 mL
Caramel (or butterscotch) ice cream topping	2/3 cup	150 mL

Place 1 banana on each tortilla. Fold in sides. Roll up tightly from bottom to enclose. Secure with wooden picks.

Combine sugar and cinnamon on small plate. Brush wrapped bananas with melted butter. Roll in sugar mixture. Arrange on baking sheet with sides. Bake in 450°F (230°C) oven for about 8 minutes until golden. Cut in half diagonally.

Whisk liqueur and chocolate spread together until smooth. Drizzle onto serving plate. Drizzle with ice cream topping. Arrange rolls over top. Serves 8.

1 serving: 303 Calories; 9.5 g Total Fat (2.4 g Mono, 0.6 g Poly, 4.5 g Sat); 15 mg Cholesterol; 52 g Carbohydrate; 2 g Fibre; 3 g Protein; 294 mg Sodium

bananas caramel

Simple ingredients come together for an impressive dessert. For a variation such as the one shown, serve this treat in dessert dishes instead of plating it.

Brown sugar, packed	1/2 cup	125 mL
Hard margarine (or butter)	1/2 cup	125 mL
Sweetened condensed milk	1/2 cup	125 mL
Corn syrup	2 tbsp.	30 mL
Medium bananas, halved lengthwise	4	4
Chopped pecans (or walnuts)	1/3 cup	75 mL

Combine first 4 ingredients in small heavy saucepan. Bring to a boil on medium. Boil for 5 minutes, stirring constantly. Remove from heat.

Place 2 banana halves on each of 4 individual sheets of heavy-duty (or double layer of regular) foil. Spoon brown sugar mixture evenly over bananas. Fold edges of foil to enclose. Preheat gas barbecue to medium. Place packets seam-side up on ungreased grill. Close lid. Cook for 8 to 10 minutes, without turning, until heated through. Transfer bananas to 4 individual plates. Drizzle with sauce from foil.

Sprinkle with pecans. Serves 4.

1 serving: 658 Calories; 35.2 g Total Fat (21.1 g Mono, 4.3 g Poly, 7.9 g Sat); 14 mg Cholesterol; 87 g Carbohydrate; 3 g Fibre; 5 g Protein; 359 mg Sodium

gooey banana fix

An indulgent pick-me-up that's ready in no time. For a no-dirty-dishes version, make a foil "dish" by scrunching the sides up and place it on a baking sheet.

Medium banana, sliced lengthwise	1	1
Milk chocolate candy bar (3 1/2 oz., 100 g, size), chopped	1/2	1/2
Caramel ice cream topping	2 tbsp.	30 mL
Miniature marshmallows	16	16

Arrange banana halves, cut-side up, in baking dish.

Sprinkle chocolate over banana halves. Drizzle with half of ice cream topping.

Randomly place marshmallows over top. Drizzle with remaining ice cream topping. Bake in 425°F (220°C) oven for 5 to 6 minutes until marshmallows are puffed and golden and chocolate is almost melted. Serves 1.

1 serving: 550 Calories; 15 g Total Fat (7 g Mono, 0.5 g Poly, 7 g Sat); 10 mg Cholesterol; 101 g Carbohydrate; 5 g Fibre; 6 g Protein; 160 mg Sodium

banana pudding parfaits

Whether you serve this as a light dessert for the family or a weekend breakfast, add the granola and banana right before serving. Swap in plain yogurt for the vanilla to make these parfaits a little less sweet.

Can of crushed pineapple	14 oz.	398 mL
Vanilla yogurt	3 cups	750 mL
Box of instant vanilla pudding powder (4-serving size)	1	1
Granola	1 cup	250 mL
Medium bananas, sliced	2	2

Drain pineapple, reserving juice in large bowl. Set aside pineapple.

Add yogurt and pudding powder to pineapple juice. Beat with whisk for about 2 minutes until mixture is smooth and thick. Add reserved pineapple. Stir well. Spoon into 6 bowls.

Sprinkle with granola. Top with banana. Serves 6.

1 serving: 356 Calories; 8.2 g Total Fat (2.3 g Mono, 3 g Poly, 2.6 g Sat); 7 mg Cholesterol; 67 g Carbohydrate; 3 g Fibre; 8 g Protein; 322 mg Sodium

frosty bananas

These fun, colourful treats can be customized with whatever coatings you like. Get creative!

Freezer pop sticks	8	8
Underripe bananas, cut in half crosswise	4	4
Semi-sweet chocolate baking squares (1 oz., 28 g, each)	8	8
Coatings (such as chocolate sprinkles, rainbow sprinkles or crushed nuts), optional		

Push freezer pop sticks about 2 inches (5 cm) lengthwise into banana halves.

Heat chocolate in small heavy saucepan on lowest heat, stirring often, until chocolate is almost melted. Do not overheat. Remove from heat. Stir until smooth. Pour into tall drinking glass until about 2/3 full. Dip 1 banana half into chocolate until completely covered. Gently rotate and pull banana out, letting excess drip back into glass. Immediately roll in desired coating. Arrange on baking sheet lined with wax paper. Repeat with remaining banana halves and coatings. Freeze, uncovered, until solid. Place in airtight container. Return to freezer. Makes 8 frosty bananas.

1 frosty banana (without coating): 210 Calories; 9 g Total Fat (0 g Mono, 0 g Poly, 6 g Sat); 0 mg Cholesterol; 32 g Carbohydrate; 4 g Fibre; 3 g Protein; 0 mg Sodium

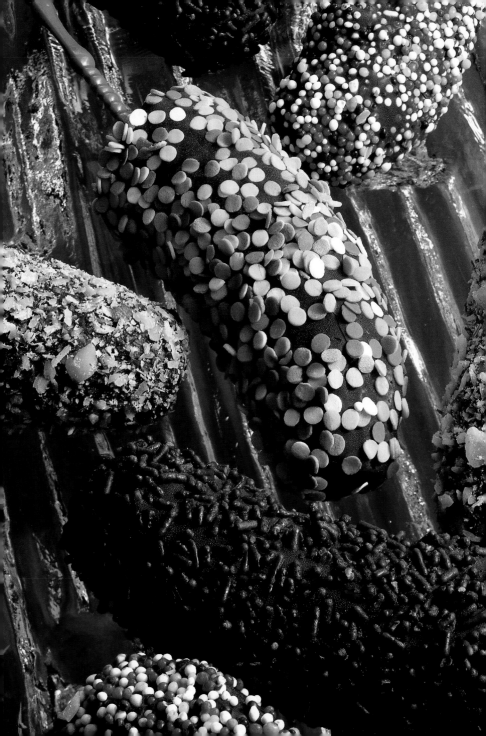

strawberry banana frozen yogurt

Light, fresh and inviting. Try this with different combinations of your favourite fruits!

Overripe medium banana, cut into 1 inch (2.5 cm) pieces	1	1
Large whole fresh strawberries	5	5
Non-fat vanilla yogurt	1 cup	250 mL
Liquid honey	1 1/2 tsp.	7 mL
Lemon juice	1 tsp.	5 mL
Vanilla extract	1/2 tsp.	2 mL
Frozen light whipped topping, thawed	1 cup	250 mL

Halved fresh strawberries or raspberries, for garnish

Arrange banana and strawberries in single layer on baking sheet. Freeze for about 2 hours until firm.

Put next 4 ingredients and frozen fruit into food processor. Process until smooth and slushy.

Fold in whipped topping. Line 9 x 9 inch (23 x 23 cm) pan with foil, extending foil over 2 sides. Pour fruit mixture into prepared pan. Freeze for about 3 hours, stirring every 30 minutes for the first 1 1/2 hours, until firm.

Garnish individual servings with strawberries. Makes about 3 1/2 cups (875 mL).

1/2 cup (125 mL): 85 Calories; 2.4 g Total Fat (trace Mono, trace Poly, 2.3 g Sat); 1 mg Cholesterol; 14 g Carbohydrate; 1 g Fibre; 2 g Protein; 32 mg Sodium

ice cream sandwiches

A summertime favourite you can make at home—no ice cream man required! No one will guess that they're homemade.

Mashed banana (about 1 large)	1/2 cup	125 mL
Peanut butter	2 tbsp.	30 mL
Chocolate chips	1 tbsp.	15 mL
Whole graham crackers	18	18
Vanilla ice cream, softened	2 cups	500 mL

Combine first 3 ingredients in small microwave-safe bowl. Microwave, covered, on high for 45 to 60 seconds until chocolate chips are almost melted. Stir until smooth.

Spread banana mixture on crackers. Arrange 9 crackers, spread-side up, in 8 x 8 inch (20 x 20 cm) pan to cover bottom.

Spread ice cream over crackers in pan. Arrange remaining crackers, spread-side down, over ice cream. Press down gently. Freeze, covered, for at least 6 hours or overnight. Cut between crackers. Makes 9 sandwiches.

1 sandwich: 217 Calories; 11.6 g Total Fat (1.7 g Mono, 0.7 g Poly, 5.8 g Sat); 53 mg Cholesterol; 24 g Carbohydrate; 1 g Fibre; 4 g Protein; 133 mg Sodium

saucy banana sundaes

The sauce can be made ahead and warmed before serving—add a bit more milk if it's too thick. For a deeper flavour use semi-sweet chocolate chips in place of milk chocolate.

Milk chocolate chips	1 cup	250 mL
Brown sugar, packed	1/2 cup	125 mL
Milk	1/4 cup	60 mL
Corn syrup	2 tbsp.	30 mL
Butter (or hard margarine)	2 tbsp.	30 mL
Vanilla extract	1/2 tsp.	2 mL
Bananas, sliced	4	4
Vanilla ice cream	1 1/2 cups	375 mL

Combine first 6 ingredients in heavy medium saucepan. Heat and stir on medium until chocolate is melted and sugar is dissolved. Bring to a boil. Remove from heat.

Place bananas in 6 dessert dishes. Scoop ice cream over banana. Spoon chocolate mixture over top. Serves 6.

1 serving: 490 Calories; 20 g Total Fat (3 g Mono, 1.5 g Poly, 11 g Sat); 25 mg Cholesterol; 77 g Carbohydrate; 4 g Fibre; 5 g Protein; 125 mg Sodium

recipe index

topical tips

Cooked grains: For recipes that call for a small amount of cooked grains, try making a larger batch and freezing the remainder for use in other recipes.

Making soured milk: If a recipe calls for buttermilk, you can substitute soured milk. To make soured milk, measure 1 tbsp. (15 mL) white vinegar or lemon juice into a 1 cup (250 mL) liquid measure. Add enough milk to make 1 cup (250 mL). Stir. Let stand for 1 minute.

Toasting nuts, seeds or coconut: Cooking times will vary for each ingredient, so never toast them together. For small amounts, place the ingredient in an ungreased frying pan. Heat on medium for 3 to 5 minutes, stirring often, until golden. For larger amounts, spread the ingredient evenly in an ungreased shallow pan. Bake in a 350°F (175°C) oven for 5 to 10 minutes, stirring or shaking often, until golden.

Zest first; juice second: When a recipe calls for grated zest and juice, it's easier to grate the fruit first, then juice it. Be careful not to grate down to the pith (white part of the peel), which is bitter and best avoided.

Nutrition Information Guidelines

Each recipe is analyzed using the Canadian Nutrient File from Health Canada, which is based on the United States Department of Agriculture (USDA) Nutrient Database.

- If more than one ingredient is listed (such as "butter or hard margarine"), or if a range is given (1–2 tsp., 5–10 mL), only the first ingredient or first amount is analyzed.

- For meat, poultry and fish, the serving size per person is based on the recommended 4 oz. (113 g) uncooked weight (without bone), which is 2–3 oz. (57–85 g) cooked weight (without bone)— approximately the size of a deck of playing cards.

- Milk used is 1% M.F. (milk fat), unless otherwise stated.

- Cooking oil used is canola oil, unless otherwise stated.

- Ingredients indicating "sprinkle," "optional" or "for garnish" are not included in the nutrition information.

- The fat in recipes and combination foods can vary greatly depending on the sources and types of fats used in each specific ingredient. For these reasons, the count of saturated, monounsaturated and polyunsaturated fats may not add up to the total fat content.